Communion and Mission

A Guide for Bishops and Pastoral Leaders on Small Church Communities

A STATEMENT FROM THE U.S. BISHOPS' COMMITTEE ON HISPANIC AFFAIRS

In May 1989, in an effort to promote Hispanic family life and to respond to the challenge posed by item number 61 of *The National Pastoral Plan for Hispanic Ministry*, the Secretariat for Hispanic Affairs sponsored a national symposium on small ecclesial communities. Forty diocesan pastoral leaders with extensive experience in the development of these communities drafted guidelines for diocesan use. These guidelines were presented for action to the Bishops' Committee on Hispanic Affairs in July 1990. A subcommittee was appointed, and several drafts were developed and revised. Final approval of the committee's statement was granted by the NCCB Administrative Committee during their meeting of March 1995 in Washington, D.C. The undersigned authorizes the publication of *Communion and Mission: A Guide for Bishops and Pastoral Leaders on Small Church Communities.*

Monsignor Dennis M. Schnurr
General Secretary
NCCB/USCC

Photo credits: cover, Catholic News Service; p. 2, *Comunidad* video; p. 13, NCCB Secretariat for Hispanic Affairs.

ISBN 1-57455-007-1

CONTENTS

PREFACE

Communion and Mission: A Guide for Bishops and Pastoral Leaders on Small Church Communities is designed as a tool for bishops and their pastoral ministers involved in the new evangelization. Given the uniqueness of the relationship between faith and culture in the diverse communities that comprise our Church in the United States, this statement seeks to shed light on the potential that small church communities can have in the efforts to promote the new evangelization, particularly in meeting the challenge of making evangelization new in its ardor, methodology, and expression.

In response to the popularity of small church communities in many Hispanic and non-Hispanic communities, the Bishops' Committee on Hispanic Affairs has developed *Communion and Mission* after several drafts and over several years. The recommendations of experienced pastoral ministers, as well as the theological context and the relationship of small communities to parish life, have been major variables in developing a statement that responds to the many pastoral challenges faced by the Church today.

Small church communities have been present in our country for many years, but in different forms and at times separated from the parish community. Perhaps this occurred because there has been little ecclesial information developed in the United States as to how to foster them, respond to their presence, or work with them in our parish communities. In recent years, however, small church communities have developed significantly. Several books and articles have been published that show how they are established and how they function within the parish community. In addition, there are well-organized diocesan, regional, and national gatherings of small church communities every year. In some dioceses, small church communities are also part of the diocesan structure and are vital to the evangelization process.

Given the diversity of the Church, small church communities are different by nature. They respond to the pastoral needs and realities of the communities of faith that form them. *Communion and Mission* underscores the common elements that are important in preserving and strengthening the Catholic identity of these communities, as well as in fostering their identity.

Communion and Mission: A Guide for Bishops and Pastoral Leaders on Small Church Communities and the accompanying bilingual discussion guide and video, *Comunidad,* can be excellent resources for the new evangelization.

Small Church Communities: A Source of Hope for the Church

Since Pentecost, the Spirit has guided the Church in each age so that it can credibly proclaim the Good News of Jesus Christ. In our time, and under the inspiration of the Spirit, a new ecclesial reality is emerging—that of small church communities—through which we can see the creative grace of God at work. Small church communities are a source of great hope for the whole Church. Steadfast, active church communities linked with the larger parish community should be encouraged and promoted. These small communities are the responsibility of the bishop, who is called to be a living sign of unity in the particular Church entrusted to his care. At this historical juncture, the Bishops' Committee on Hispanic Affairs offers the following reflections to assist the diocesan bishops and their collaborators as they offer leadership and guidance to the small church communities in their dioceses.

Among Hispanics, small church communities are becoming an important and useful vehicle for the new evangelization to which the Church is being called.[1] They are a place in which the religious and cultural identity of Hispanics is affirmed. In addition, the Christian household is a privileged place in which persons relate a faith journey, find nurturing support, and focus on missionary efforts. The strong sense of family which Hispanics retain in their daily living is strengthened in the small church communities.

When solidly rooted in Scripture, church tradition, and Hispanic religiosity, small church communities constitute a new moment in the Church's self-understanding, epitomizing the celebration and proclamation of the Church. These gatherings of the People of God are integrally linked to the parish, and through it, to the diocesan and universal Church.

Today's active communities are works in progress. They have yet to reach their full potential to become authentic community centers of evangelization. This great potential exists, however, since small church communities already engage in personal relationships of faith through fellowship, evangelization, liturgy, mission, and service.

Hispanics and Small Church Communities

For Hispanics, a predominant Catholic presence in the United States,[2] the Catholic faith is closely linked with cultural manifestations of their identity. Small church communities help to affirm the Hispanics' faith-cultural identity on a personal level and provoke a communal evangelical mission. In this way Hispanics continue to contribute as a religious force to the Church and society.

Through small church communities, Latino Catholics are finding a way to preserve and share the rich cultural and faith expressions and family values that help them face the challenges of a rapidly changing world. Small church communities strengthen Hispanic religiosity—a homespun spirituality that enables them to take responsibility for their Christian way of living. The Church respects this emerging spirituality as a reflection of Hispanic cultural and spiritual identity and recognizes that an attack against this identity is an attack against their Catholicity.

Small communities fortify a centuries-old tradition of faith. Affirmed and strengthened in their identity as Catholics, Hispanics can better serve the larger community. Yet, while small communities serve to preserve a vibrant faith, they are not simply warehouses of religious and cultural traditions. They are truly the expression of an emerging spirituality.

In the last few years, they have made significant strides in the religious, educational, political, economic, and social areas of our society. Hispanics are more visible in church leadership as bishops, theologians, and lay leaders. They have become a visible presence in this country's political, economic, and educational systems. Nevertheless, they still rank among the poorest Americans on the economic scale. They are represented disproportionately in the numbers of high school dropouts, pregnant teenagers, and persons in prison.

While many Latinos have not yet found a home in our society, they have generally found one in the Church, especially in small church communities. Many Hispanic Catholics are more comfortable with small communities where people know one another and can interact with their priests and ministers on a personal level. Hispanics look to these communities for a credible experience of evangelization, where the Gospel is preached and truly lived in daily life.

COMMUNION AND MISSION

The origin of the Church lies in the mission of Jesus Christ, the Incarnate Son. In him and through him, the life of the Trinity is communicated. The community of disciples saw themselves sent by God into history with the mission of Christ in the power of the Spirit.[3] Thus, the small faith communities model is taken from the Church's foundation, the primary community *par excellence*—the Trinity. As Church, the small communities are "a people made one with the unity of the Father, the Son, and the Holy Spirit."[4] At the heart of this unity is the Church's mission of bringing the promises of God to fulfillment.

Since the beginning, the Church has recognized itself as communitarian (Acts 2:42). A small church community, by nature, is a communion with a mission. This belief is grounded in the truth that the mystery of God and the mystery of salvation are inseparable. God's self-emptying love, which draws us into life with the Trinity, is lived out in his saving deeds among us. It is a way of living the mystery that is the Church. As groups with a mission, small church communities realize the trinitarian relationships and God's saving activity among us.

The Triune God invites us to communion. Jesus Christ incarnates this invitation, initiating the reign of God among us. Some reject this invitation, while those who accept it share in God's glory.[5] Small church communities respond to this invitation through their efforts to form authentic communion as Church and through their mission of fostering the reign of God. The Spirit enlightens them so that they can understand Jesus' message. This Spirit reveals to them the true identity of Christ and empowers them for the mission. Since this communion also invites them to include others, giving preference always to the rejected, marginalized, abandoned, and forgotten, the Church is renewed in its self-expression as communion for all. This basic sense of communion enables the Church to authenticate itself by seeing itself in a new light.

Partaking of life in the Triune God has dramatic consequences. It means entering, in the most profound sense, into God's saving project for a new humanity. Living in communion with the Triune God calls members of these communities to enter into a life of love and communion with all their brothers and sisters. In this sense, small communities—communally and prophetically—live out the call as artisans of the coming reign of God.

Integral evangelization is at the core of the faith life of the small communities:

> There is no gap between love of neighbor and the desire for justice. . . . The evil inequities and oppression of every kind which afflict millions of men and women today openly contradict Christ's Gospel and cannot leave the conscience of any Christian indifferent.
>
> The Church, in her docility to the Spirit, goes forward faithfully along the paths to authentic liberation. . . . But a vast number of Christians, from the time of the Apostles onwards, have committed their powers and their lives to liberation from every form of oppression and to the promotion of human dignity. The experience of the saints and the example of so many works of service to one's neighbor are an incentive and a beacon for the liberating undertakings that are needed today.[6]

In their efforts to bring God's providential plan to fulfillment, small communities are confronting obstacles to communion with God and with one another, dictating a re-ordering of life at all levels. They work to triumph over the social, political, economic, racial, gender, and environmental relationships that humanity creates as tools for destruction and death. This struggle against the obstacles that are contemporary society's idols of death serves to renew the small communities, which are not set up for themselves, but for mission.[7]

Small church communities should not be isolated from the rest of the Church's life. The Church is not simply a community of communities. It is an organic whole that expresses itself in ways such as small communities. While these structures are local and particular, their reality is universal and truly Catholic. So is their thrust. As realizations of the mystery of the Church, small church communities do not exist separately from the apostolic ministry of the bishops. Small communities ultimately attest to the faithfulness of God's relationship with us and with our world.

CHARACTERISTICS OF SMALL CHURCH COMMUNITIES

The following constitutive elements are common to many authentic small church communities throughout the country. These characteristics can serve as a guide in working with newly formed church communities or in getting to know those communities already in place. It is our sincere hope that by supporting all church communities, they will continue to mature and bear fruit.

1. Composition

Small church communities allow their members to relate to one another at a personal level, sharing in their common journeys of faith. Their small size reflects an attempt at a qualitative, rather than quantitative, approach to faith development. This allows greater emphasis on a person's lived experience as seen through the lens of church tradition, sacred Scripture, and the Hispanic history of suffering and hope.

The smallness of the group allows for concentration of church life and mission. It is not an effort for separation from the parish. The strength of the small groups comes from a concerted effort to delve more deeply into Christian life on a more personal level, while at the same time remaining intimately linked to the Church's universal mission. In a small group the experience of God's daily effect on life stands at the center of the group's activities. Knowing firsthand the needs of its members allows participants to experience a sense of belonging and interconnectedness with their co-journeyers. The small gathering enables a more direct faith formation and personal sharing of stories of God's saving deeds.

2. Communitarian Life

In a society plagued by individualism, separatism, and a general disregard for the well-being of others, small church communities reinforce the communitarian nature of church life. By calling their members to make the connection between faith and daily life, small ecclesial communities can credibly live out the Church's preferential option for the poor through their close links with the homeless, the poor, and those suffering at the bottom of the unjust social pyramid.

The essence of church life in the Christian community is to become one with the Trinity through communion with one another. Living in community is to live in communion with the Triune God. God is present where there is authentic communion. A life of communion and love with our brothers and sisters is the path to divine life.

The sharing of faith stories reinforces the experience that Christian life is communitarian. Reading and meditating upon the sacred Scriptures in community helps us to understand the meaning of Scripture with the mind of the Church, thus avoiding individualistic and erroneous interpretations. This leads to a renewed link with the Christian tradition and a deeper understanding of the Church as *koinonia*.[8]

Through a communitarian life, all members are challenged to a shared vision of the life and work of Jesus Christ and the call to imitate him with a view of service to the world. The group aims for authentic community, which is centered on life with God and the mission of bringing the world to full unity in him. Although the Christian community is called to be of one mind (Acts 2:46), differences and conflicts are bound to arise. Living in community, however, calls all to deal creatively with tensions in obedience to the unfolding plan of God. Overcoming difficulties brings new life and depth to each member of the community.

The communitarian life of small church communities invites its members to full life and growth in God. These communities are not simply associations for intimate self-disclosure and emotional support. They promote their members' growth through the experiences and processes in which they discover and accept their God-given vocation. In keeping with the mission of the Church, they become artisans of their own destiny.

In communities people come together to authenticate their interactions and to share in the struggles of their journeys. The communitarian lifestyle, however, poses challenges for its members. In our busy society, small groupings become reflective environs, raising the question of God's saving deeds in our lives and our world. The challenge of living in community is to enlarge a person's vision of God's saving plan without undermining one's development and growth. Individuals can feel accepted, welcomed, and invited to maturity.

The community does not close in on itself, but rather integrates families of grandparents, parents, sisters, and brothers. It promotes strong interpersonal relationships based on faith, love, and unity. Members share their daily lives, their basic problems, their joys, and their struggles. All feel welcomed there—integrated and co-responsible—with a fundamental equality, even if there is a diversity of function. Members of the community demonstrate a mutual, profound, caring, loving, and committed partnership that brings them together in solidarity.

Small ecclesial communities can avoid the trap of being self serving through a grounding in their mission and through interconnection with other levels of Church. The communitarian aspect strongly emphasizes this unity as an essential element of being Church. This unity forms a bridge with other communities, allowing the mission of God to flourish.

The communion that God desires does not end with the small church community. It reaches out to other levels of church life, including the parish, the diocese, the region, and the universal Church. Small ecclesial communities are in communion with these other elements, as well as with their legitimate pastors. They participate in a strong *pastoral de conjunto*.[9]

3. Ecclesial Role

Small church communities are a communion of God's people living out the mission of Jesus Christ in the power of the Spirit. In these communities, new and effective ways of living the mystery of the Church are being formed. This phenomenon challenges us to look at ourselves as Church. Since it is still too early to know where this movement of the Spirit will lead us, we can only point to the reality and offer constructive direction.

The numbers of small church communities emerging within parishes indicate that parishes are providing pastoral leadership and fostering credible structures. For this we are grateful to their pastors and pastoral leaders and to God who gives the growth. Other parishes could also benefit greatly from the presence of small church communities. Without parish support and proper leadership, small groups could arise but lose direction. Furthermore, fundamentalist groups could easily move in to fill a vacuum.

Small church communities must not be seen in isolation. They are not another Church, but part of the one Church. Their major contribution is the new expression of Christian life. They offer the Church a new inner life. Small communities are not a new movement in the Church. Nor are they simply neighborhood subgroups of the parish structure. They are the Church itself. They are a smaller expression of the universal Church. As such, the Church is developing new structures to allow this inner life to flourish. As communities of faith and mission, they give witness to a renewal of the Church's inner life. Where this will lead depends on the Spirit.

Pope John Paul II has called for new parish structures for the Christian faithful. He calls for "adaptation of parish structures according to the full flexibility granted by canon law . . . in promoting participation of the lay faithful," and sees small communities as "true expressions of ecclesial communion" when united with their pastors.[10] These vibrant small communities allow Catholics to regain their universal momentum at a local level.

Small church communities understand their ecclesial nature as they strive to balance their inner life with their missionary thrust. Without this effort they run the risk of losing their credibility as ecclesial communities. Evangelization in all its dimensions enables the communities to blossom and remain on the path of constant renewal in faithfulness to Christ.

4. *Prophetic Mission*

Our God is a God of life. As prophet, Jesus announced and initiated God's life as the rule of his coming reign among us. Small communities are called to make as their own Jesus' prophetic vision of the coming reign. Like Jesus, they must stand in solidarity with all who suffer. Thus, it is important that these communities study the Church's social teachings and remain open to living in solidarity with the poor. As small prophetic communities, they exist in the concrete realities of daily life, announcing the reign of God's new life.

In their commitment to fostering the reign of the Triune God, small church communities experience the mystery of God and the mystery of salvation as inseparable. As prophetic communities their task is to examine human reality from the perspective of God's purposes so that their efforts are connected to God's designs for a new humanity.

Small church communities critically investigate the root causes of the idols of death, which are the obstacles to God's plan. They also interpret the signs of the times from the view of the mission of Jesus. Therefore, when small communities discuss, plan, and focus on what direction to take, they begin and end with their commitment to the task of the coming reign of God. In this way, these church communities become faithful to Christ's mission by refusing to give idols of death a place in history. As prophetic communities, they confront sin as an annihilation of communion with God and with one another.

Since God's plan for us is communion, small church communities are seen as countercultural in a society torn by division. The profound alienation felt in today's society is tied to the root cause of sin masquerading itself in the form of injustice, marginalization, abuse, abortion, drugs, and violence. The communities' task of integral evangelization is to view people in all of the dimensions affecting their lives: spiritual, political, cultural, economic, social, educational, and environmental, among others. In this way they can proclaim Christ as true Lord of all creation.

Bonding together under the banner of the God of life, small communities can critically examine the prevailing culture. They support an alternative way of life in a materialistic and consumption-driven society. The tendencies toward individualism and separatism and the disregard for the good of others are challenged by the presence of prophetic communities. Small communities invite and help people to be different in society, calling them to a conversion to the ways of God. This leads to communion.

As prophetic church communities, these groups attest to the possibilities of a new life with the Triune God, bearing witness from the very place where the Gospel is lived. They profess communally that God is for us. Small communities affirm the faithfulness and truthfulness of God's relationship with us and with our world. For this reason, we can call them communities of hope. As such, they proclaim that the God of life is victorious over all the forces of destruction that threaten true communion between sisters and brothers, among themselves, and with the Triune God.

Latinos resonate with the prophetic dimension of small church communities because they have often lived as strangers in their own land. Yet, they have remained united by a profound faith and hope in the providence of God. In spite of historical obstacles, faith is at the center of their lives. Hispanics are experiencing a reawakening of cultural identity which is, at the same time, a rebirth of faith identity. Small faith communities affirm what is inherently good about being an Hispanic Catholic, while at the same time challenging members to grow in light of the Church's universal mission.

5. *Liturgical Life*

The life of the Church is directed to the worship and praise of the living God. Worship and praise are, therefore, an essential part of living in small church communities. In this worship, the Eucharist is the heart of their life and their essential link with the unity of the whole Church. Life in service to the reign of God is connected intimately with praise of God. The Eucharist celebrates the paschal mystery—the communion of God with his people—and anticipates the table of the new humanity where all will be one in Christ (Jn 17). It is the summit toward which all is focused and the source of all new life.[11] The eucharistic life of the small communities is inseparable from their commitment to partake in the mission of God's saving plan. The members bring to the Eucharist their lives as Christians to offer as a part of worship. They become renewed in their commitment to begin again as agents of the reign of God.

These small assemblies gather as a people of praise and lift up to God key moments in their common journey of joys and struggles. They celebrate in prayers of thanksgiving and petition. While they share in personal devotions, community prayer unites the group with the prayerful chorus of the whole Church. As assemblies of praise, they are centers for celebrating the gift of faith and the promise of new life.

In light of their evangelical mission, it is important for small worshiping communities to develop prayer lifestyles and forms of communal reflection in keeping with the Church's tradition and practice. In so doing, the Bible is primary among their sources. Special sensitivity must be given to the inclusion of the faith traditions and customs of all the members present. Inculturation is indispensable in order to make the people's faith expressions a part of their prayer life. In this way, people touch the mystery of faith in their own language and through their own symbols. They are thus led to a renewed commitment to Christian living.

Hispanics tend to view all of life as sacred and have generally developed a profound sense of the divine in daily living. This is evident in their popular religiosity. Unfortunately, liturgical celebrations reflecting the Hispanic life of faith and other events that are dear to them, such as Guadalupe celebrations, *posadas*, processions, and *quinceañeras*, are often not incorporated into the worship life of the parish. In small communities, Hispanics find support to retrieve this sense of popular piety and to reaffirm the values contained in these celebrations. As a people of praise, Latinos have a profound sense of celebration, or fiesta, and view life as a victory of grace over sin. Fiesta celebrates a moment of God's presence among us and anticipates the joy of the coming reign of God.

6. Missionary Thrust

As the Father has sent me, so I send you (Jn 17:18). Small church communities are fundamentally missionary agents of the reign of God. The Second Vatican Council stressed the notion of the Church as missionary to the world. In more recent times, Pope John Paul II emphasized the right of all peoples to hear the Good News and called the Church to a new evangelization in preparation for the third millennium of faith.

Small church communities engage in evangelization as an ongoing process, with life in a missionary community calling the members to constant conversion. This implies an encounter with Christ and an openness to allowing the reign of God to penetrate and guide one's whole life. To remain faithful to any evangelization effort, missionary church communities need to make solidarity with the poor a priority. This helps the community endure and retain sight of its ultimate goal of communion and mission. A community matures by being missionary; otherwise, it becomes self-serving and self-destructive.

Missionary communities assess how best to concretely live out their evangelical mission by critically studying the causes of alienation, emptiness, and suffering. They question why society supports obstacles to God's plan. As missionary church communities, they challenge the causes of individualism, separatism, and death-dealing ideologies that masquerade as being for the good of others. Small church communities protest all that attacks the coming reign of God. They plan as a group, within the framework of a *pastoral de conjunto*, to more effectively respond to the needs of the people with whom they live. Their efforts attest to God's activity to eradicate sin and death and form a communion where all are brothers and sisters in union with the Triune God.

7. Ministerial Role

Small church communities are ministerial because they are made up of baptized persons who are called to be collaborators in the priesthood of Jesus Christ.

> Christ, the high priest and unique mediator, has made of the Church "a kingdom of priests for his God and Father" (Rev 1:6;

cf. Rev 5:9-10; 1 Pt 2:5, 9). The whole community of believers is, as such, priestly. The faithful exercise their baptismal priesthood through their participation, each according to his proper vocation, in Christ's mission as priest, prophet, and king. Through the sacraments of Baptism and Confirmation the faithful are "consecrated to be . . . a holy priesthood" (LG 10, 1).[12]

Through the Church God calls forth its ministers and forms them into ministerial communities. They exercise their role by linking the new evangelization with efforts to manifest among us the saving work of Jesus Christ, the high priest. Seen from this perspective, communities call their members to assume their rightful role in the mission of the whole Church. In this way, the laity will move from seeing themselves as simply father's helpers to seeing themselves as responsible collaborators in the life and mission of the ministerial community. The more the faithful fulfill their work in the home, the parish, the neighborhood, and the world, the more they make present the saving work of Christ, the high priest.

While all members belong to the ministerial community through baptism, confirmation, and Eucharist, not everything that the community does is considered ministry. The community engages in authentic ministry when its members' activities are carried out for the sake of the reign of God and in the name of the Church. Ministry is directly tied to the saving work of Christ. For this reason, communities should offer their members proper and adequate training and formation. Ministries will flourish and new ones will emerge as long as members creatively collaborate with their pastors, so that all ministry is done in the name of the Church.

> A rapidly growing phenomenon in the young churches . . . is that of "ecclesial basic communities." . . . They . . . become leaven of Christian life, of care for the poor and neglected, and of commitment to the transformation of society. Within them, the individual Christian experiences community and therefore senses that he or she is playing an active role and is encouraged to share in the common task. Thus, these communities become means of evangelization and of the initial proclamation of the Gospel and a source of new ministries.[13]

In affirmation of the hierarchical nature of the Church, small communities foster a discipleship in solidarity and equal responsibility. According to their proper call and mission, all ministers have the duty to make present the vision and work of Jesus Christ, the priest, prophet, and king.[14]

Ministry is a call, a vocation. Small church communities call their members to promote vocations for all the church ministries. Members involved in ministerial activity are not volunteers who simply help the Church or the clergy, but are responsible disciples participating in the ministry of Christ, the high priest.

Conclusion

The elements outlined above are not an exhaustive list of the characteristics of small church communities. Others will emerge as these communities continue to bear fruit. We single these out simply to highlight certain characteristics of church life that will bind us as one Church. In these basic elements we see factors that renew the Church in a way that makes all of us more credible and at the same time faithful to the Lord. We offer guidance to help small church communities mature as an integral part of the universal Church, especially in light of the new evangelization.

Ultimately, communion and mission are a gift of the Triune God. It is the Father who offers us this gift in the person of Jesus Christ and by the power of the Spirit. It is the Triune God who brings into life these small communities and who sustains them. It is this Spirit of the living God who again calls the Church to credibility in communion and mission, bearing witness to God's faithfulness to us and to our world. As Mary was present at Pentecost with the original church community, may she, model of faithful discipleship, continue to challenge and inspire the small ecclesial communities to bear much fruit.

QUESTIONS FOR EVALUATING SMALL CHURCH COMMUNITIES

The following questions can serve as a guide for small church communities. They may be used for the self-evaluation that each community should conduct from time to time. They may also be used by the pastor (or bishop) when he makes a pastoral visit to a community. Finally, the questions may serve as a guide in the formation of new communities: the questions can be addressed as the community develops each of its constitutive elements.

1. *Composition*

The small size of communities allows their members to relate on a personal level and help to develop interconnectedness and belonging. The smallness of the group encourages concentration of church life and mission, not separation from the larger church community.

a. How do members get to know each other in community?
b. How do members become integrated into this community? Is it by an evangelization retreat or a personal invitation? Are they part of a neighborhood grouping or a section of a parish?
c. What is the composition of the group? Who is included (youth, elderly, etc.)?
d. How do people experience a sense of belonging in this small community?
e. How do members get to know the needs of the persons in the community and in the larger parish community?

f. How committed are the members to each other?
g. What type of sharing occurs in the group? Is personal faith shared? Is it focused on Christ and his mission? Do members tell stories of God in their lives?
h. Who is the facilitator? How is this person selected? Is the selection done in consultation with the pastor and parish council?
i. How are the members helped to articulate their personal faith journey and their call to participate in the mission of Christ to build the reign of God?

2. Communitarian Life

The communitarian aspect of small communities reinforces a strong tradition of community in church life. A communal lifestyle challenges the members to a shared vision of Jesus' life and work.

a. How do the members help each other understand the group's role in the mission of Christ?
b. How do the community's members relate their faith to their daily lives?
c. How does the group help each member become a mature adult Christian?
d. How does the group help its members discover a common purpose in applying gospel values to all aspects of their lives?
e. What values does the group hold in common?
f. How are the members called to deeper faith?
g. How is the Bible used in the group's gatherings?
h Is there an environment in the community that encourages ongoing conversion and constant refocusing on the group's mission?
i. How does the community demonstrate care and concern for the needs of its members?
j. Who participates in the *pastoral de conjunto*?
k. How are the gifts of the members being used to strengthen the life and work of the community?
l. How does the community resolve conflicts among its members?
m. How does the group deal with diversity?

3. Ecclesial Role

Small communities are Church and should not exist in isolation from the parish and diocese. They are not another Church, but are part of the one Church, offering new expressions and new inner life.

a. How is the small community linked with the parish community?
b. How does the group share its experiences with other communities?
c. How are the bishop, pastor, parish pastoral leader, and parish council connected to the small community?
d. How many times do the parish/diocesan leaders visit the community?
e. Are the parish leaders members of small communities?
f. What type of relationship does the small community have with other parish groups?
g. What type of leadership does the group need?
h. How does the group express its openness to the movement of the Spirit in the Church?
i. How is the small community a sign of the presence of Christ in the world?
j. Give examples that show how the community is maturing as Church.
k. How are the group members contributing to the life and ongoing renewal of the Church?
l. Are members clear about their mission? What is the group's understanding of the mission of Jesus in today's world?
m. How are activities coordinated? How does the group handle evaluations of its members and the group's mission efforts?
n. How do the members promote the domestic Church?

4. Prophetic Mission

Small church communities are prophetic when they proclaim that God's ways lead to communion with God and one another. They are prophetic when they give witness to the possibilities of new life with the Triune God.

a. What are the community's efforts toward integral evangelization? How does the community evangelize?
b. How does the group witness as artisans of God's new humanity?
c. How are the members enabled to articulate gospel values for themselves so that each gives witness to God's coming reign?
d. How does the community plan to give direction to its prophetic stance as a countercultural community and servant to the reign of God?
e. How does the community analyze problems in the neighborhood or city in light of the mission of the Church to foster the reign of peace and justice?
f. How are members trained to critically assess any obstacles to God's plans?
g. What efforts are made to reach out to the alienated Catholic, to the marginalized in society, to rejected members of society?
h. What type of formation is offered to members regarding the social teachings of the Church?
i. How does the community make present the saving work of Jesus Christ?
j. How does the community offer hope to the world?

5. Liturgical Life

Life in service to the reign of God is connected intimately with praise of God. Inculturation in the liturgy is instrumental to express the Hispanic sense of the sacredness of daily life.

a. How does the community relate its mission to its worship?
b. What is the prayer life of the community?
c. How does the group incorporate the Hispanic popular religious traditions into its prayer and worship?
d. Are services celebrated in Spanish? If necessary, are the services held bilingually?
e. How is the community sensitive to the cultural backgrounds of its members, and how is this expressed in worship?
f. Do all members of the community help in the liturgical

preparations for special occasions such as *quinceañeras*, weddings, baptisms, and *posadas?*

g. Does the community participate in the sacramental preparation of its members: baptism, first communion, marriage?
h. What provisions are made to incorporate children, youth, the elderly, and the physically disabled in the prayer life of the Church?
i. Does the community have an appropriate setting for prayer (*altarcitos*, religious symbols)?
j. When does the community gather to celebrate and pray with other communities? With the larger parish community?
k. How does the group prepare to participate in the parish's liturgical life?
l. What type of scripture reflection is used in the small community?
m. When does the group have *fiesta*?
n. How often does the community go on retreat?
o. Who organizes the calendar of celebrations for the community?
p. How are members helped to discover the sacredness of life in ordinary life experiences?

6. Missionary Thrust

Small communities are missionary agents for the reign of God. They make the Church's option for the poor a priority in their missionary efforts.

a. How are the members called to conversion? Retreats, workshops, missions?
b. In what way does the community relate conversion to Christ with the mission of Christ?
c. How is the group in solidarity with the poor?
d. How does the community reach out to those who have not yet heard about Christ?
e. How does the community plan and formulate goals to give direction to its missionary efforts?
f. How does the group assess its faithfulness to Christ?

7. *Ministerial Role*

Small communities foster the active participation of their members as collaborators in the priesthood of Jesus Christ. The main thrust of all ministry is the reign of God.

a. How are the gifts of the members called forth in community?
b. How are the gifts of the community placed at the service of the neighborhood and parish?
c. How are the members trained to be ministers and leaders? In the community, in the parish, in the diocese? What type of training is being offered?
d. Do all ministers work in collaboration with the pastor and parish pastoral leaders?
e. What efforts are made to foster vocations to the priesthood, religious life, and to all other parish ministries?
f. How is the role of women in the communities respected?
g. What is done in the community to develop a serious commitment to ministry?
h. What is being done in the community to help members move from an attitude of being simply father's helpers and parish volunteers to being responsible collaborators in the life of the Church?

A Suggested Model for Gatherings

The structure for these gatherings varies depending on the region of the country, the liturgical season, the number of years the group has been together, and so forth.

Welcome

Prayer of Praise and Hymns

Scripture Reflection or a Teaching

Group Sharing on the Reflection or Teaching (as it applies to their faith journey in light of the Church's mission)

Prayers of the Faithful

Our Father

Announcements and Other Community Concerns

Closing Prayers and Hymns

Hospitality

NOTES

1. The experience of small communities among Hispanics/ Latinos in the United States is different from the Latin American experience of *comunidades de base*. In the United States, Hispanic Catholics are a minority in a Protestant country, often experiencing cultural and linguistic alienation. Since U.S. Hispanics have forged intimate ties between their identity and their faith expressions, small church communities serve to affirm their faith and cultural identity.

   The rich Latin American experience of small base communities called for in Medellin, Puebla, and Santo Domingo will continue to enrich the discussion and formation of the Church in the Americas. Furthermore, the experience of Hispanic Catholics in small church communities can be a help to others in this country in the formation of these communities.

2. National Conference of Catholic Bishops, *Hispanic Presence: Challenge and Commitment* (Washington, D.C.: United States Catholic Conference Publishing Services, 1983); *National Pastoral Plan for Hispanic Ministry* (Washington, D.C.: United States Catholic Conference Publishing Services, 1987).

3. Vatican Council II, *Dogmatic Constitution on the Church* (Washington, D.C.: United States Catholic Conference Publishing Services, 1964), 2-4; Eph 2:18.

4. The expression is from St. Cyprian's *De Oratione Dominica* 23: Pl 4, 553, and is quoted in the *Dogmatic Constitution on the Church*, 4.

5. "He came to what was his own, but his own people did not accept him. But to those who did accept him he gave power to become children of God . . ." (Jn 1:11-12).

6. Congregation for the Doctrine of the Faith, *Instruction on Christian Freedom and Liberation* (Vatican City: Vatican Polyglot Press, 1986), 57.

7. Paul VI, *On Evangelization in the Modern World* (Washington, D.C.: United States Catholic Conference Publishing Services, 1975). In number 58, Paul VI calls the small communities to be in solidarity with the Church's life, nourished by its teachings and united with its pastors.

8. Acts 2:42-44; 2 Cor 13:13.

9. *National Pastoral Plan for Hispanic Ministry* (Washington, D.C.: United States Catholic Conference Publishing Services, 1987), 9-17.

10. John Paul II, *The Lay Members of Christ's Faithful People* (Washington, D.C.: United States Catholic Conference Publishing Services, 1988), 26.

11. Vatican Council II, *Constitution on the Sacred Liturgy* (Washington, D.C.: United States Catholic Conference Publishing Services, 1963) 10.

12. *Catechism of the Catholic Church* (Washington, D.C.: United States Catholic Conference Publishing Services, 1994), 1546.

13. John Paul II, *On the Permanent Validity of the Church's Missionary Mandate* (Washington, D.C.: United States Catholic Conference Publishing Services, 1990), 51.

14. *Catechism of the Catholic Church* (Washington, D.C.: United States Catholic Conference Publishing Services, 1994), 1268.

To order additional copies of *Communion and Mission* (publication no. 5–007), a copy of the complementary video *Comunidad* (video no. 5–008), or to obtain a catalog of other USCC titles, call toll-free 1-800-235-8722. In the Washington metropolitan area or from outside the United States, call 301-209-9020.

Comunión Y Misión

Orientaciones para Obispos y Agentes de Pastoral Sobre Pequeñas Comunidades Eclesiales

UNA DECLARACIÓN DEL
COMITÉ DE OBISPOS PARA
ASUNTOS HISPANOS

En mayo de 1989, con el propósito de afirmar la vida familiar hispana y para responder al desafío propuesto en el número 61 del Plan Pastoral Nacional para el Ministerio Hispano, el Secretariado para Asuntos Hispanos auspició un diálogo nacional sobre las pequeñas comunidades eclesiales. Cuarenta agentes pastorales diocesanos compartieron su gran experiencia de trabajo en estas comunidades señalando pautas para uso diocesano. Estas pautas fueron presentadas al Comité de Obispos para Asuntos Hispanos, en julio de 1990. Este nombró un subcomité y se desarrollaron y revisaron varios borradores. La Declaración del Comité de Obispos para Asuntos Hispanos, fue aprobada por el Comité Administrativo de la Conferencia Nacional de Obispos Católicos (NCCB), durante su reunión de Marzo 1995, en Washington, D.C. Por consiguiente, el suscrito autoriza la publicación de Comunión y Misión: Orientaciones sobre Pequeñas Comunidades Eclesiales para Obispos y Agentes Pastorales.

Monseñor Dennis M. Schnurr
Secretario General
NCCB/USCC

Fotos: portada, Catholic News Service; página 2, *Comunidad*; página 13, Secretariado de Asuntos Hispanos.

Las citas bíblicas fueron tomadas de la Biblia Latinoamericana, Editorial Verbo Divino, 1989.

ISBN 1-54755-007-1

CONTENIDO

PREFACIO

Comunión y Misión: Orientaciones para Obispos y Agentes de Pastoral es un instrumento para el uso de los obispos y agentes de pastoral involucrados en la Nueva Evangelización. Debido a la singularidad de la relación entre fe y cultura de las diversas comunidades que comprenden la Iglesia en los Estados Unidos, esta declaración busca dar a conocer el potencial que pueden tener las pequeñas comunidades eclesiales en la Nueva Evangelización, particularmente al enfrentar el desafío de hacer la evangelización nueva en su ardor, metodología y su expresión.

Como respuesta al florecimiento de las pequeñas comunidades eclesiales en las comunidades hispanas y no-hispanas y después de haber redactado varios borradores durante los últimos años, el Comité de Obispos para Asuntos Hispanos ha desarrollado el documento Comunión y Misión. También se tomaron en cuenta las recomendaciones de agentes de pastoral y las preocupaciones manifestadas por los obispos respecto al contexto teológico de la declaración, así como la relación de las pequeñas comunidades con la vida parroquial.

Las pequeñas comunidades eclesiales han estado presentes en este país por muchos años, en diferentes modalidades y muchas veces separadas de la vida de la parroquia. Quizás haya sido por la falta de información de parte de la Iglesia en los Estados Unidos en como responder a esta presencia y promoverla o como hacerla parte integral de la comunidad parroquial. En los últimos años y debido al aumento de las pequeñas comunidades eclesiales, se han publicado libros y artículos que señalan como promover estas comunidades y cómo funcionan dentro de la parroquia. También se celebran reuniones anuales tanto a nivel diocesano como regional y nacional sobre estas pequeñas comunidades. En algunas de las diócesis, la pequeña comunidad eclesial es parte de la estructura diocesana y es vital en el proceso de evangelización.

Debido a la diversidad de la Iglesia, las pequeñas comunidades son diferentes en naturaleza y así deben ser. Ellas responden a la realidad y necesidades de la comunidad que la forman, particularmente en su contexto de fe y cultura, lo cual es de suma importancia para el bienestar y

efectividad de la comunidad. De igual manera, *Comunión y Misión* presenta elementos básicos para mantener la identidad católica de estas comunidades, su identidad de parroquia y su unión a la vida parroquial.

Comunión y Misión: Orientaciones para los Obispos y Agentes de Pastoral sobre Pequeñas Comunidades Eclesiales y el material bilingüe de la guía de discusión y el video *Comunidad*, pueden ser excelentes recursos en la Nueva Evangelización.

Pequeñas Comunidades Eclesiales: Fuentes de Esperanza para la Iglesia

A partir de Pentecostés, el Espíritu ha guiado a la Iglesia en cada época para que con credibilidad proclame la Buena Nueva de Jesucristo. En nuestros tiempos, y bajo la inspiración del Espíritu, está surgiendo una nueva realidad eclesial: la de las pequeñas comunidades eclesiales. Por ellas podemos ver la labor de la gracia creativa de Dios. Las pequeñas comunidades eclesiales son fuente de gran esperanza para toda la Iglesia. Las comunidades eclesiales, activamente ligadas a la comunidad parroquial, deben ser estimuladas y promovidas con empeño. Estas pequeñas comunidades son responsabilidad del obispo, quien está llamado a ser signo vivo de unidad en la Iglesia particular confiada a su cuidado. En esta coyuntura histórica, el Comité Episcopal para Asuntos Hispanos ofrece las siguientes reflexiones para asistir a los obispos diocesanos y a sus colaboradores en la labor de liderazgo y orientación de las pequeñas comunidades eclesiales en sus respectivas diócesis.

Las pequeñas comunidades eclesiales se están convirtiendo, entre hispanos, en un importante y útil vehículo para la nueva evangelización a la que la Iglesia es llamada.[1] La identidad cultural y religiosa de los hispanos es afirmada en estas comunidades. Así como el hogar cristiano es el lugar privilegiado donde sus miembros comparten su caminar en la fe, donde encuentran apoyo vital, y donde concentran su labor misionera, así también el poderoso sentido de familia que los hispanos conservan en su vida diaria, se hace más fuerte aún en las pequeñas comunidades eclesiales.

Cuando se enraizan sólidamente en la Escritura, en la Tradición de la Iglesia y en la religiosidad hispana, las pequeñas comunidades eclesiales constituyen un nuevo momento de autocomprensión para la Iglesia, encarnando asi la celebración y proclamación de la misma Iglesia.

Estas comunidades del pueblo de Dios están ligadas integralmente a la parroquia y, a través de ella, a la Iglesia diocesana y universal.

Las comunidades de hoy son obras en desarrollo. Tienen que llegar todavía a la plenitud de su potencial como auténticos centros

y comunidades de evangelización. Este gran potencial ya comenzó a darse, sin embargo, ya que las pequeñas comunidades eclesiales están comprometidas en relaciones interpersonales de fe a través del compañerismo, de la evangelización, de la liturgia, de la misión y del servicio.

La experiencia que los hispanos católicos han tenido en pequeñas comunidades eclesiales, a lo largo y ancho de la nación, podría ser utilizada como un modelo por otras comunidades católicas que desean desarrollar pequeñas comunidades eclesiales.

Los Hispanos y las Pequeñas Comunidades Eclesiales

Para los hispanos, presencia católica predominante en los Estados Unidos,[2] la fe católica está estrechamente ligada a manifestaciones de su identidad. Las pequeñas comunidades eclesiales ayudan a afirmar y

sostener la identidad religiosa y cultural del hispano, a nivel personal, promoviendo también su misión evangélica en la comunidad. De este modo los hispanos contribuyen como fuerza religiosa tanto a la Iglesia como a la sociedad.

En las pequeñas comunidades eclesiales los hispanos hallan el modo de preservar y compartir su riqueza cultural y religiosa, y valores familiares que les permiten enfrentarse a los desafíos de un mundo en rápido proceso de cambio. Las pequeñas comunidades eclesiales fortalecen la religiosidad hispana: espiritualidad aprendida en familia que les lleva a asumir la vida cristiana con responsabilidad. La Iglesia respeta esta espiritualidad como reflejo que es de la identidad cultural y espiritual hispana, y reconoce que cualquier afrenta contra esta identidad es una afrenta a su catolicidad.

Las pequeñas comunidades eclesiales refuerzan una multisecular tradición de fe. Los hispanos podrán servir mejor en sociedad si se les afirma y apoya su identidad como católicos. Pero aunque las pequeñas comunidades sirven para preservar la fe viva, no son meros almacenes de tradiciones religiosas y culturales. Son verdaderas expresiones de una nueva espiritualidad.

En los últimos años estas comunidades han contribuído avances de importancia en los campos religioso, educativo, político, económico y social de nuestra sociedad. Los hispanos se han hecho más visibles en posiciones de liderazgo en la Iglesia como obispos, teólogos y líderes laicos. Se han vuelto presencia constatable en el sistema político, económico y educativo. Y sin embargo, continúan estando entre los americanos más pobres en la escala económica. Están desproporcionadamente representados en estadísticas de deserción escolar, de embarazos de adolescentes y de personas en prisión.

Aunque muchos latinos no han encontrado todavía su lugar en nuestra sociedad, casi siempre han hallado un hogar en la Iglesia, especialmente en las pequeñas comunidades. Muchos católicos hispanos se sienten más a gusto en pequeñas comunidades donde la gente se conoce y donde pueden relacionarse con sus sacerdotes y ministros de modo más personal. Los hispanos se dirigen a estas comunidades en busca de una experiencia creible de evangelización, donde el evangelio sea predicado y donde se le viva de verdad en la vida diaria.

Comunión y Misión

El origen de la Iglesia descansa sobre la misión de Jesucristo, el Hijo encarnado. En él y por él se nos comunica la vida de la Trinidad. La comunidad de los discípulos se entendió a si misma como enviada por Dios al interior de la historia, con la misma misión de Cristo y el poder del Espíritu.[3] De ahí que el modelo de la pequeña comunidad de fe se tome del fundamento mismo de la Iglesia: la Trinidad como comunidad primaria por excelencia. Como Iglesia, las pequeñas comunidades son "un pueblo reunido en la unidad del Padre, del Hijo y del Espiritu Santo."[4] En el corazón de esta unidad se encuentra la misión de la Iglesia: llevar a su cumplimiento las promesas de Dios.

Desde el principio la Iglesia se ha reconocido a sí misma como comunitaria (Hch 2:42). Una pequeña comunidad eclesial es, por su propia naturaleza, una comunión con una misión. Esto se basa en la verdad de que el misterio de Dios y el misterio de la salvación son inseparables. Dios vive en sus obras salvíficas su amor generoso que nos atrae a la vida trinitaria. Es un modo de vivir el misterio que es la Iglesia. Como grupos con una misión, las pequeñas comunidades eclesiales hacen presente las relaciones trinitarias y la actividad salvífica de Dios entre nosotros.

El Dios trino nos invita a la comunión. Jesucristo encarna esta invitación, inaugurando el reino de Dios entre nosotros. Algunos rechazan esta invitación en tanto que quienes la aceptan comparten la gloria de Dios.[5] Las pequeñas comunidades eclesiales responden a este llamado fomentando la auténtica comunión como Iglesia y promoviendo el reino de Dios. El Espíritu las ilumina para que puedan entender el mensaje de Jesús. Este mismo Espíritu les revela la verdadera identidad de Cristo y les da fuerza para la misión. Puesto que esta comunión conduce a la inclusión de otros, dando siempre preferencia a los rechazados, a los marginados, y a los abandonados y olvidados, la Iglesia se renueva en su auto-expresión como comunión de todos y para todos. Este sentido básico de comunión le da a la Iglesia la posibilidad de autenticarse a si misma al verse bajo nueva luz.

La participación en la vida trinitaria de Dios tiene profundas consecuencias. Significa entrar, en el sentido más hondo, en el proyecto salvífico de Dios a favor de una nueva humanidad. Vivos en la comu-

nión con el Dios trino, los miembros de estas comunidades son llamados a una vida de amor y comunión con todos sus hermanos y hermanas. En este sentido las pequeñas comunidades viven, comunitaria y proféticamente, la vocación de los artesanos del reino de Dios que se aproxima.

La evangelización integral está al centro de esta vida de fe de las pequeñas comunidades:

> No hay distancia alguna entre al amor al prójimo y la lucha por la justicia. . . Las perversas desigualdades y opresiones de varios tipos que hoy afligen a millones de hombres y mujeres contradicen abiertamente al evangelio de Cristo y no pueden dejar indiferente la conciencia de ningún cristiano.
>
> La Iglesia, en su docilidad al Espíritu, avanza con fidelidad por el camino de la liberación auténtica. . . Innumerables cristianos, desde los tiempos de los Apóstoles, han comprometido sus fuerzas y sus vidas a favor de la liberación de toda forma de opresión y a favor de la promoción de la dignidad humana. La experiencia de los santos y el ejemplo de tantas obras al servicio de nuestros prójimos son incentivo y orientación para la labor liberadora que el presente exige.[6]

En su esfuerzo por cumplir el plan providencial de Dios, las pequeñas comunidades enfrentan obstáculos a la comunión con Dios y con los demás. Esto les exige que reordenen su vida a todo nivel. Las comunidades luchan por sobreponerse a relaciones sociales, políticas, económicas, raciales, de género y ambientales que la humanidad crea como armas de destrucción y muerte. La lucha contra estos ídolos de muerte, creados por la sociedad contemporanea, sirve para renovar a las pequeñas comunidades. Estas no han sido hechas para sí mismas sino para cumplir una misión.[7]

Las pequeñas comunidades eclesiales no deben aislarse del resto de la vida de la Iglesia. La Iglesia no es simplemente una comunidad de comunidades. Es un todo orgánico que se expresa de diversas formas, como en las pequeñas comunidades. Si bien estas estructuras son locales y particulares, su realidad es universal y verdaderamente

católica. Como también lo es su impulso. Como realizaciones del misterio de la Iglesia, las pequeñas comunidades no existen separadamente del ministerio apostólico de los obispos. Las pequeñas comunidades dan testimonio de la relación fiel de Dios con nosotros y con nuestro mundo.

Elementos Constitutivos de las Pequeñas Comunidades Eclesiales

Los siguientes elementos constitutivos son comunes a muchas de las auténticas pequeñas comunidades eclesiales a lo largo y ancho del país. Estas características pueden servir para orientar el trabajo con comunidades eclesiales recién formadas, o para conocer mejor comunidades ya existentes. Nuestra sincera esperanza es que al querer apoyar a todas las comunidades eclesiales éstas sigan madurando y dando fruto.

1. Composición

Las pequeñas comunidades eclesiales permiten a sus miembros relacionarse entre sí a nivel interpersonal, compartiendo su caminar en la fe. El pequeño tamaño del grupo refleja un enfoque más cualitativo que cuantitativo en el desarrollo de la fe. Esto permite un mayor énfasis en la experiencia viva de las personas, vistas a través del prisma de la Tradición de la Iglesia, de las Sagradas Escrituras y de la historia hispana de sufrimiento y esperanza.

Lo reducido del grupo permite el concentrarse en la vida y en la misión de la Iglesia. No se trata de separarse de la parroquia. El poder de los pequeños grupos les viene precisamente del énfasis que les permite penetrar más profundamente en la vida cristiana a nivel personal, haciéndoles a su vez permanecer más íntimamente ligados a la misión universal de la Iglesia. En un grupo pequeño la experiencia de la presencia activa de Dios en la vida cotidiana se coloca en el mismo centro de las actividades del grupo. Conociendo de primera mano las necesidades de los demás miembros de la comunidad hace que los participantes se sientan unidos a sus compañeros de grupo. La pequeña reunión permite a los miembros una formación más directa en la fe, llevándoles a compartir entre ellos testimonios de lo que Dios hace a su favor.

2. Vida comunitaria

Las pequeñas comunidades eclesiales enfatizan la naturaleza comunitaria de la vida de la Iglesia en medio de esta sociedad plagada de individualismo, divisiones y desinterés general por el bienestar de los demás. Al convocar a sus miembros a conectar su fe con su vida diaria, las pequeñas comunidades eclesiales viven creiblemente la opción preferencial de la Iglesia por los pobres. Esta conexión se ha de dar en estrecha relación entre las comunidades y los que no tienen casa, con los pobres y con quienes soportan sobre sus espaldas el peso de la injusta pirámide social.

Lo esencial de la vida de Iglesia en la comunidad cristiana es llegar a hacerse uno con la Trinidad mediante la comunión con los prójimos. Vivir en comunidad es vivir en comunión con el Dios trino. Dios esta presente allí donde hay auténtica comunión. Una vida de comunión y de amor con nuestros hermanos y hermanas es el camino seguro hacia la vida divina.

Compartir testimonios de fe refuerza la experiencia de que la vida cristiana es comunitaria. La lectura y la meditación de las Sagradas Escrituras en comunidad nos ayudan a entender, con la mente de la Iglesia, el significado de la Escritura, evitando así interpretaciones individualistas y equivocadas. El resultado será un renovado encuentro con la tradición cristiana y un entendimiento más profundo de la Iglesia como *koinonía*.[8]

A través de la vida comunitaria todos los miembros del grupo son retados a compartir su visión de la vida y misión de Jesucristo, y todos son llamados a imitarlo en su actitud de servicio al mundo. El grupo busca ser una comunidad auténtica, centrada en la vida con Dios y en la misión que busca llevar al mundo a la unidad plena en Dios. Y aunque la comunidad cristiana está llamada a ser de un solo pensar (Hch 2:46), es comprensible que surjan diferencias y conflictos. La vida comunitaria nos llama a hacerles frente a las tensiones con creatividad y en obediencia al Dios que se revela. La superación de las dificultades otorga nueva vida y más profundidad a cada miembro de la comunidad.

La vida compartida en las pequeñas comunidades eclesiales invita a sus miembros a una vida más plena y a crecer en Dios. Estas

comunidades no son simples asociaciones para el desahogo íntimo y el apoyo emocional. Ellas más bien promueven el crecimiento de sus miembros por medio de experiencias y procesos en los que descubren y aceptan la vocación a la que Dios les llama. Unidos a la misión de la Iglesia, los miembros de estas comunidades se convierten en artesanos de su propio destino.

La gente se reune en comunidad para autenticar sus relaciones y para compartir sus luchas y proyectos. La vida comunitaria, sin embargo, desafía a los miembros del grupo. En nuestra sociedad siempre ocupada, los pequeños grupos son espacios de reflexión que nos enfrentan a los gestos salvíficos de Dios en nuestra vida y en nuestro mundo. El reto de la vida comunitaria es cómo ampliar la visión que se tiene del plan salvífico de Dios sin frustrar el desarrollo y crecimiento personales. En comunidad, las personas son aceptadas, acogidas e invitadas a madurar.

La comunidad no se cierra en sí misma, sino que une a familias de abuelos, papás, mamás y hermanos. Promueve relaciones interpersonales fuertes basadas en la fe, el amor y la unidad. Los miembros comparten su vida diaria, sus principales problemas, sus alegrías y sus luchas. Todos se sienten acogidos aquí, integrados y corresponsables, en igualdad fundamental, aun existiendo una diversidad de funciones. Los miembros de la comunidad demuestran un compañerismo mutuo, profundo, acogedor, cariñoso y comprometido que les reune en solidaridad.

Las pequeñas comunidades eclesiales pueden evitar caer en la trampa de servirse a sí mismas si se fundamentan en la misión y si se relacionan con los otros niveles de la Iglesia. El aspecto comunitario claramente enfatiza la unidad como elemento esencial del ser Iglesia. Esta unidad forma un puente con otras comunidades y permite que se desarrolle la misión de Dios.

La comunión que Dios desea no se agota con la pequeña comunidad eclesial. Alcanza otros niveles de la vida de la Iglesia también, incluyendo la parroquia, la diócesis, la región y la Iglesia universal. Las pequeñas comunidades eclesiales están en comunión con estos otros niveles y con sus pastores legítimos. Ellas participan en la *pastoral de conjunto*.[9]

3. Dimensión Eclesial

Las pequeñas comunidades eclesiales son comunión del pueblo de Dios que vive la misión de Jesucristo en el poder del Espíritu. Nuevos modos de vivir efectivamente el misterio de la Iglesia se van descubriendo en las comunidades. Este fenómeno nos desafía a mirarnos como Iglesia. Siendo todavía muy pronto para saber hacia dónde nos llevará este impulso del Espíritu, podemos apenas señalar esta realidad y sugerir alguna orientación constructiva.

El número de pequeñas comunidades eclesiales que están surgiendo en las parroquias sugiere que las parroquias están ofreciendo liderazgo pastoral y promoviendo estructuras creíbles. Por esto damos las gracias a los párrocos y a los agentes de pastoral, y a Dios que da el crecimiento. Otras parroquias pueden beneficiarse también con la presencia de pequeñas comunidades eclesiales. Sin el apoyo de la parroquia y sin un liderazgo adecuado, grupos pequeños pueden surgir pero podrían perder la dirección. Es más, grupos fundamentalistas podrían fácilmente venir a llenar el vacío.

Las pequeñas comunidades eclesiales no deben ser vistas en aislamiento. Ellas no son otra iglesia, sino parte de la única Iglesia. Su mayor contribución es ser una nueva expresión de la vida cristiana. Ellas ofrecen a la Iglesia una nueva vida interior. Las pequeñas comunidades no son un movimiento nuevo en la Iglesia. No son tampoco simples subgrupos de vecinos dentro de la estructura parrroquial. Son la Iglesia misma. Son una expresión más pequeña de la Iglesia universal. Por consiguiente, la Iglesia está desarrollando nuevas estructuras para hacer que florezca su vida interior. Como comunidades de fe y misión, ellas dan testimonio de la renovación de la vida interior de la Iglesia. Hacia dónde nos llevará esto depende del Espíritu.

El papa Juan Pablo II ha lanzado un llamado para crear nuevas estructuras parroquiales para los fieles cristianos. Nos pide. . . "adaptar las estructuras parroquiales de acuerdo con la flexibilidad plena que concede el derecho canónico. . . para promover la participación de los fieles laicos." El papa ve a las pequeñas comunidades como "expresiones verdaderas de comunión" cuando están unidas a sus pastores.[10] Las vibrantes pequeñas comunidades permiten a los católicos recobrar el impulso universal a nivel local.

Las pequeñas comunidades eclesiales entienden su naturaleza eclesial cuando intentan balancear su vida interior con su ímpetu misionero. Sin este intento correrían el riesgo de perder credibilidad como comunidades eclesiales. La evangelización, en todas sus dimensiones, hace que estas comunidades florezcan y permanezcan en el camino de constante renovación en su fidelidad a Cristo.

4. Misión Profética

Nuestro Dios es un Dios de vida. Como profeta, Jesús anunció y dispuso que la vida divina fuera norma del reino que se acerca a nosotros. Las pequeñas comunidades están llamadas a hacer suya la visión profética de Jesús sobre el reino que viene. Como Jesús, ellas deben ser solidarias con todo el que sufre. Por eso es importante que las comunidades estudien la doctrina social de la Iglesia y estén dispuestas a vivir solidariamente con los pobres. Como pequeñas comunidades proféticas, ellas existen en medio de las realidades concretas de la vida diaria, anunciando ahí la vida nueva del reino de Dios.

En su compromiso por promover el reino del Dios trino, las pequeñas comunidades eclesiales experimentan el misterio de Dios y el misterio de salvación como inseparables. Como comunidades proféticas su labor es examinar la realidad humana desde la perspectiva del plan de Dios de manera que sus esfuerzos estén conectados con los designios de Dios para una nueva humanidad.

Las pequeñas comunidades eclesiales analizan críticamente los orígenes de los ídolos de muerte, que son obstáculos al plan de Dios. También interpretan los signos de los tiempos desde la perspectiva de la misión de Jesús. Por lo tanto, el compromiso con las tareas del reino de Dios que se aproxima es el inicio y fin del proceso por el que las pequeñas comunidades discuten, planifican y deciden qué dirección tomar. De este modo las pequeñas comunidades eclesiales, fieles a la misión de Cristo, rehusan dar a los ídolos de muerte un lugar en la historia. Como comunidades proféticas, enfrentan al pecado como destrucción de la comunión con Dios y con el prójimo.

Puesto que el plan de Dios para nosotros es la comunión, las pequeñas comunidades eclesiales son vistas como contra-culturales en una sociedad desgarrada por la división. La profunda alienación

presente en la sociedad actual tiene su raíz en el pecado que se disfraza de injusticia, marginación, abuso, aborto, drogas y violencia. Es tarea de la evangelización integral considerar a las personas en todas las dimensiones que afectan su vida: espiritual, política, cultural, económica, social, educativa y ambiental, entre otras. Así podrán las comunidades proclamar a Cristo como verdadero Señor de toda la creación.

Reunidas bajo el estandarte del Dios de la vida, las pequeñas comunidades pueden examinar críticamente la cultura prevalente. Ellas promueven una propuesta alternativa de vida en medio de la sociedad materialista y consumista. La presencia de comunidades proféticas desafía la tendencia hacia el individualismo y el separatismo así como al desprecio por el bienestar de los demás. Las pequeñas comunidades convocan y ayudan a la gente a ser diferentes en la sociedad, invitándoles a convertirse a los caminos de Dios. Esto lleva a la comunión.

Como comunidades eclesiales proféticas, estos grupos dan testimonio de las posibilidades de vida nueva con el Dios trino, y lo hacen desde donde se vive el evangelio. Ellas profesan comunitariamente que Dios está con nosotros. Afirman que la relación de Dios con nosotros y con nuestro mundo es fiel y confiable. Por esta razón podemos llamarlas comunidades de esperanza. Y como tales proclaman que el Dios de la vida vence a las fuerzas de destrucción que amenazan a la verdadera comunión entre los hermanos y con el mismo Dios.

Los latinos sintonizan con la dimensión profética de las pequeñas comunidades eclesiales porque frecuentemente ellos mismos han vivido como extranjeros en su propia tierra. A pesar de todo, la gente ha permanecido unida por medio de su profunda fe y de su esperanza en la providencia de Dios. Pese a los obstáculos puestos por la historia, la fe está al centro de sus vidas. Los hispanos hoy experimentan un nuevo despertar de identidad cultural que es también el renacer de su identidad católica. Las pequeñas comunidades de fe afirman lo que es inherentemente bueno en la realidad del católico hispano en cuanto tal, a la vez que desafían a sus miembros hacia un mayor crecimiento a la luz de la misión universal de la Iglesia.

5. *Vida Litúrgica*

La vida de la Iglesia se dirige a adorar y alabar al Dios vivo. Adoración y alabanza son, por consiguiente, elementos fundamentales de la vida de las pequeñas comunidades eclesiales. La eucaristía es el corazón de su vida y de su unión esencial con la Iglesia entera. El servicio al reino de Dios está íntimamente ligado a la alabanza a Dios. La eucaristía celebra el misterio pascual: la comunión de Dios con su pueblo, anticipando así la mesa común de la nueva humanidad donde todos seremos uno en Cristo (Jn 17). Es la cima hacia la cual todo se orienta, y la fuente de toda vida nueva.[11] La vida eucarística de las pequeñas comunidades es inseparable de su compromiso de participación en la misión del plan salvífico de Dios. Los miembros traen sus vidas cristianas a la eucaristía para ofrecerlas como parte del culto, saliendo renovados como agentes del reino de Dios.

Estas pequeñas asambleas reunen a la gente como pueblo para la alabanza. Así elevan a Dios los momentos claves de su común experiencia, llena de alegrías y dificultades. En comunidad la gente eleva oraciones de acción de gracias y de petición. Aunque también compartan devociones personales, la oración de la comunidad une al grupo con el coro orante de toda la Iglesia. Como asambleas de alabanza estas comunidades son espacios para la celebración del don de la fe y de la promesa de una vida nueva.

En vista a su misión evangélica, es importante que las pequeñas comunidades desarrollen estilos de oración y de reflexión comunitaria en sintonía con la Tradición y la práctica de la Iglesia. La Biblia es por eso el principal recurso para ese fin. Debe haber un especial respeto para con las tradiciones de fe y las costumbres de los miembros presentes, integrándolas a la oración y reflexión comunitarias. La inculturación es indispensable para hacer que las expresiones de fe de la gente sean parte de su vida de oración.[12] Asi la gente se aproximará al misterio de fe en su propio lenguaje y mediante sus propios símbolos, llegando a un renovado compromiso con la vida cristiana.

Los hispanos tienden a mirar la vida toda como sagrada, habiendo desarrollado un profundo sentido de lo divino en la vida diaria. Esto

es evidente en su religiosidad popular. Desafortunadamente, celebraciones litúrgicas que reflejen su fe y los momentos sobresalientes de su vida comunitaria y familiar (como las celebraciones de Guadalupe, posadas navideñas, procesiones y quinceañeras) son rara vez incorporadas a la vida litúrgica total de la parroquia. En las pequeñas comunidades, los hispanos encuentran el apoyo necesario para rescatar su propio sentido de piedad popular y para reafirmar los valores contenidos en estas celebraciones. Como pueblo llamado a la alabanza, los latinos tienen un sentido profundo de celebración y fiesta, viendo a la vida como victoria de gracia sobre el pecado. La fiesta celebra un momento de presencia de Dios entre nosotros y anticipa la alegría del reino de Dios que se acerca.

6. Impetu Misionero

"Como el Padre me ha enviado, así los envío yo" (Jn 17:18). Las pequeñas comunidades eclesiales son, fundamentalmente, agentes misioneros del reino de Dios. El Concilio Vaticano II enfatizó la idea de la Iglesia como misionera en el mundo. Más recientemente el papa Juan Pablo II recalcó el derecho de todos los pueblos a escuchar la Buena Nueva,[13] convocando a la Iglesia a una nueva evangelización en preparación al tercer milenio de la fe.

Para las pequeñas comunidades eclesiales la evangelización es un proceso permanente. La realidad misionera de la comunidad llama a los miembros a la conversión continuada. Esto implica encuentro con Cristo y apertura al reino de Dios, de modo que este penetre y guíe la vida toda. A fin de permanecer fiel a la evangelización, toda comunidad misionera tiene que privilegiar la solidaridad con los pobres. Así la comunidad mantendrá viva la visión de su meta última: comunión y misión. La comunidad avanzará en madurez si es misionera; de lo contrario se ensimismará y auto-destruirá.

El análisis crítico de las causas de la alienación, del vacío interno y del sufrimiento es el camino certero por el que las comunidades misioneras descubren cómo mejor vivir la misión evangélica en lo concreto de todos los días. Por este medio también cuestionan porque la sociedad pone obstáculos al plan de Dios, y enfrentan las causas del individualismo, del separatismo y de las ideologías de muerte que se disfrazan de bien. Las pequeñas comunidades eclesiales protestan contra todo aquello que sea afrenta al reino de Dios. En el marco de la *pastoral de conjunto*, cada comunidad planifica cómo responder con eficacia a las necesidades del pueblo con el que comparte la vida. El esfuerzo de la comunidad es testimonio del Dios que actúa para erradicar el pecado y la muerte y para formar una comunión donde todos sean hermanos en unión con el Dios trino.

7. Dimensión Ministerial

Las pequeñas comunidades eclesiales son ministeriales porque sus miembros son bautizados, llamados a ser colaboradores en el sacerdocio de Jesucristo.

> Cristo, sumo sacerdote y único mediador, ha hecho de la Iglesia "un reino de sacerdotes para su Dios y Padre" (Ap 1:6; cf. Ap 5:9-10; 1Pe 2:5,9). Toda la comunidad de los creyentes es, como tal, sacerdotal. Los fieles ejercen su sacerdocio bautismal a través de su participación, cada uno según su vocación propia, en la misión de Cristo, Sacerdote, Profeta y Rey. Por los sacramentos del bautismo y la confirmación los fieles son "consagrados para ser...un sacerdocio santo" (LG 10,1).[14]

Por medio de la Iglesia Dios llama a sus ministros y los hace comunidades ministeriales. Los ministros llevan a cabo su misión ligando la nueva evangelización con iniciativas que manifiesten entre nosotros la obra salvífica de Jesucristo el Sumo Sacerdote. Desde esta perspectiva cada comunidad llama a sus miembros a asumir el papel que les corresponde en la misión de la Iglesia toda. De esta forma los laicos dejarán de pensar que son apenas ayudantes de los sacerdotes y pasarán a ser colaboradores corresponsables de la vida y de la misión de la comunidad ministerial. Cuanto más cumplan los fieles su misión en el hogar, en la parroquia, en el barrio y en el mundo, tanto más harán presente la obra salvífica de Cristo el Sumo Sacerdote.

Si bien todos los miembros pertenecen a la comunidad ministerial por el bautismo, la confirmación y la eucaristía, no todo lo que la comunidad hace se consideraría ministerio. Hay ministerio auténtico cuando los miembros de la comunidad actúan a favor del reino de Dios y en nombre de la Iglesia. El ministerio está directamente ligado a la obra salvífica de Cristo. Por esta razón cada comunidad debe ofrecer a sus miembros el entrenamiento y la formación correctos y adecuados. Florecerán los ministerios y otros nuevos surgirán si los miembros de la pequeña comunidad eclesial colaboran creativamente con sus pastores, para que todo ministerio sea hecho en nombre de la Iglesia.

> Un fenómeno en rápido crecimiento en las iglesias jóvenes. . . es el de las "comunidades eclesiales de base". . . ellas. . . son fermento de vida cristiana, de cuidado a los pobres y olvidados, y de compromiso con la transformación de la sociedad. En ellas el cristiano experimenta comunidad, sintiendo así que juega un papel activo, animado a participar en la tarea común. De esta manera estas comunidades se convierten en medios de evangelización y de proclamación primera del evangelio. Son fuente de nuevos ministerios.[15]

Afirmando la naturaleza jerárquica de la Iglesia, las pequeñas comunidades promueven el discipulado en solidaridad y corresponsabilidad. Según su propia vocación y misión, todos los ministros

deben hacer presentes la visión y la obra de Jesucristo Sacerdote, Profeta y Rey.[16]

El ministerio es un llamado, una vocación. Las pequeñas comunidades eclesiales llaman a sus miembros a promover vocaciones para todos los ministerios de la Iglesia. Los que sirven a la comunidad en alguna actividad ministerial no son meros voluntarios que prestan ayuda a la Iglesia o al clero. Son realmente discípulos responsables que participan en el ministerio de Cristo, Sumo Sacerdote.

Conclusión

Los elementos que hemos discutido no agotan todas las posibles características de las pequeñas comunidades eclesiales. Otros surgirán conforme estas comunidades sigan dando fruto. Hemos enumerado estos simplemente para subrayar ciertos aspectos de la vida eclesial que nos unen en Iglesia. En estos elementos hallamos factores que renuevan a la Iglesia haciéndola más creíble a la vez que nos hacen a todos más fieles al Señor. Hemos ofrecido estas orientaciones con el propósito de ayudar a las pequeñas comunidades eclesiales a madurar como parte integral de la Iglesia universal, especialmente a la luz de la nueva evangelización.

En última instancia, tanto la comunión como la misión son don del Dios trino. Es el Padre el que nos ofrece este don en la persona de Jesucristo por el poder del Espíritu. Es el Dios trino quien da vida y sostiene a estas pequeñas comunidades. Es el Espíritu del Dios vivo quien de nuevo llama a la Iglesia a una mayor credibilidad en comunión y misión, dando testimonio de la fidelidad de Dios para con nosotros y nuestro mundo. Y así como María estuvo en Pentecostés con la primitiva comunidad eclesial, quiera ella que es modelo de discipulado fiel, seguir impulsando e inspirando a las pequeñas comunidades eclesiales para que den fruto abundante.

Preguntas para Evaluación de Pequeñas Comunidades Eclesiales

Las siguientes preguntas pueden servir como orientación para pequeñas comunidades eclesiales. Pueden usarse para la autoevaluación que cada comunidad debe hacer de vez en cuando. Pueden ser usadas también por el párroco (o por el obispo) cuando haga la visita pastoral a la pequeña comunidad. O pueden servir de orientación para la formación de nuevas comunidades. Las preguntas pueden hacerse conforme cada comunidad vaya desarrollando sus elementos constitutivos.

1. Composición

El pequeño tamaño de cada comunidad ayuda a que sus miembros se relacionen y comuniquen entre sí a nivel personal, y promueve el desarrollo del sentido de pertenencia. Lo reducido del grupo anima a concentrarse en la vida y misión de la Iglesia, y no a separarse del resto de la Iglesia.

a. ¿Cómo es que los miembros de la comunidad llegan a conocerse entre sí?
b. ¿Cómo es que se integran nuevos miembros a esta comunidad? ¿A través de un retiro de evangelización o por invitación personal? ¿Son parte de un grupo de vecinos o de una sección de la parroquia?
c. ¿Cuál es la composición del grupo? ¿Quiénes lo componen (jóvenes, ancianos, etc.)?
d. ¿Cómo es que los participantes sienten que realmente pertenecen a esta pequeña comunidad?
e. ¿Cómo hacen los participantes para conocer las necesidades de los otros miembros de la comunidad y de la comunidad parroquial toda?
f. ¿Qué tan comprometidos están los miembros unos con otros?
g. ¿Cómo es que la gente comparte en este grupo? ¿Se comparte la fe personal? ¿Esta fe se centra en Cristo y en su misión? ¿Los miembros dan testimonios de lo que Dios va haciendo en sus vidas?

h. ¿Quién es el animador? ¿Cómo fue seleccionado? ¿Se hizo la selección tras consultar con el párroco y el consejo parroquial?
i. ¿Cómo es que se ayuda a los miembros de la comunidad a articular su caminar personal en la fe y su participación en la misión de construcción del reino de Dios?

2. Vida Comunitaria

La dimensión comunitaria en las pequeñas comunidades recalca la sólida tradición comunitaria en la vida de la Iglesia. El estilo de vida comunitaria exige que se tenga una visión compartida de la vida y de la obra de Jesús.

a. ¿Cómo es que los miembros de la comunidad se ayudan entre sí para entender su papel en la misión de Cristo?
b. ¿Cómo es que relacionan la fe con su vida diaria?
c. ¿Cómo es que el grupo ayuda a cada uno de sus miembros a ser cristianos adultos y maduros?
d. ¿Cómo es que el grupo ayuda a descubrir metas comunes cuando se aplican valores evangélicos a la vida diaria en toda su complejidad?
e. ¿Cuáles son los valores que el grupo cree tener en común?
f. ¿Cómo es que el grupo llama a sus miembros a una fe más profunda?
g. ¿Cómo se usa la Biblia en las reuniones del grupo?
h. ¿Hay en la comunidad un ambiente que estimule la conversión continuada y el reencuentro frecuente con la misión del grupo?
i. ¿Cómo es que la comunidad muestra su cuidado y preocupación por las necesidades de cada uno de sus miembros?
j. ¿Quién participa en la *pastoral de conjunto*?
k. ¿Cómo es que se aprovechan los talentos de cada miembro del grupo para fortalecer la vida y el trabajo de la comunidad?
l. ¿Cómo es que la comunidad resuelve conflictos entre sus miembros?
m. ¿Cómo es que la comunidad se enfrenta a la diversidad?

3. Dimensión Eclesial

Las pequeñas comunidades son Iglesia y no deben existir aisladas de la parroquia y de la diócesis. No son otra Iglesia sino parte de la única Iglesia a la que ofrecen nuevas expresiones y nueva vida interior.

a. ¿Cómo es que la pequeña comunidad se relaciona con la comunidad parroquial?
b. ¿Cómo es que el grupo comparte sus experiencias con otras comunidades?
c. ¿Cómo se relacionan el obispo, el párroco, los demás agentes de pastoral y el consejo parroquial con la pequeña comunidad eclesial?
d. ¿Con qué frecuencia o regularidad visitan a la comunidad los líderes de la parroquia o de la diócesis?
e. ¿Los líderes parroquiales son miembros de pequeñas comunidades?
f. ¿Qué tipo de relación mantiene la pequeña comunidad con otros grupos parroquiales?
g. ¿Qué tipo de liderazgo necesita el grupo?
h. ¿Cómo expresa el grupo su apertura a la acción del Espíritu en la Iglesia?
i. ¿Cómo es que la pequeña comunidad da testimonio de la presencia de Cristo en el mundo?
j. Dar ejemplos que muestren cómo está madurando la comunidad como Iglesia.
k. ¿Cómo es que los miembros del grupo van contribuyendo a la vida de la Iglesia y a su renovación continuada?
l. ¿Tienen los miembros claridad acerca de su misión? ¿Qué entiende el grupo que es la misión de Jesús en el mundo actual?
m. ¿Cómo se coordinan las actividades? ¿Cómo maneja el grupo la evaluación de sus miembros y de los esfuerzos misioneros del grupo?
n. ¿De qué manera promueven los miembros del grupo a la Iglesia doméstica?

4. Misión Profética

Las pequeñas comunidades eclesiales son proféticas cuando proclaman que los caminos de Dios conducen a la comunión con Dios y con el prójimo. Son proféticas cuando dan testimonio de nueva vida con el Dios trino.

a. ¿Qué esfuerzos de la comunidad se dirigen a la evangelización integral? ¿De qué manera es que la comunidad evangeliza?
b. ¿Cómo es que el grupo da testimonio de ser artesanos de la nueva humanidad?
c. ¿Cómo es que el grupo promueve entre sus miembros la articulación adecuada de los valores del evangelio de modo que cada uno de testimonio del reino de Dios que se acerca?
d. ¿Cómo es que el grupo espera poder actuar proféticamente como comunidad contracultural, servidora del reino de Dios?
e. ¿Cómo es que la comunidad analiza los problemas de su barrio y ciudad a la luz de la misión de la Iglesia, para promover el reino de paz y justicia?
f. ¿Cómo es que la comunidad entrena a sus miembros para analizar críticamente los obstáculos que la sociedad interpone frente a la voluntad de Dios?
g. ¿Qué hace la comunidad para acercarse a los católicos alejados, a los marginados de la sociedad, y a los despreciados por la sociedad?
h. ¿Qué tipo de formación sobre la doctrina social de la Iglesia ofrece la comunidad a sus miembros?
i. ¿Cómo es que la comunidad hace presente la obra salvífica de Jesucristo?
j. ¿Cómo es que la comunidad le ofrece esperanza al mundo?

5. Vida Litúrgica

El servicio al reino de Dios está íntimamente ligado a la alabanza de Dios. La inculturación de la liturgia es necesaria para expresar el sentido hispano de lo sagrado en la vida diaria.

a. ¿Cómo es que la comunidad relaciona su misión con el culto?
b. ¿Cómo es la vida de oración de la comunidad?
c. ¿Cómo es que el grupo incorpora las tradiciones religiosas populares hispanas a su oración y culto?
d. ¿Se celebran servicios litúrgicos en español? Si fueran necesarios, ¿se celebran también servicios litúrgicos bilingües?
e. ¿Cómo es que la comunidad muestra sensibilidad a las culturas de sus miembros, y cómo es que expresa esa sensibilidad y esas culturas en el culto?
f. ¿Todos los miembros de la comunidad colaboran en la preparación de celebraciones litúrgicas para ocasiones especiales tales como quinceañeras, bodas, bautismos y posadas navideñas?
g. ¿Participa la comunidad en la preparación pre-sacramental de sus miembros: para el bautismo, la primera comunión, el matrimonio?
h. ¿Qué medidas se han tomado para asegurar la participación de niños, jóvenes, ancianos y de impedidos en la vida de oración de la Iglesia?
i. ¿La comunidad dispone de un ambiente apropiado para la oración (altarcitos, símbolos religiosos)?
j. ¿Cuándo es que se reune la comunidad para celebrar y orar con otras comunidades? ¿Y con el resto de la comunidad parroquial?
k. ¿Cómo es que el grupo se prepara para participar en la vida litúrgica de la parroquia?
l. ¿Qué tipo de reflexión bíblica es usada en la pequeña comunidad?
m. ¿Cuándo es que el grupo celebra fiestas?
n. ¿Con qué frecuencia es que la comunidad hace algún retiro?
o. ¿Quién organiza el calendario de celebraciones de la comunidad?
p. ¿Cómo es que la comunidad ayuda a sus miembros a descubrir el valor sagrado de la vida en la realidad de todos los días?

6. Impetu Misionero

Las pequeñas comunidades son agentes misioneros del reino de Dios. La opción de la Iglesia por los pobres es una prioridad en sus empeños misioneros.

a. ¿Cómo es que la comunidad llama a sus miembros a la conversión? ¿Retiros, talleres, misiones?
b. ¿Cómo es que la comunidad liga la conversión a Cristo a la misión de Cristo?
c. ¿Cómo es que el grupo se solidariza con los pobres?
d. ¿Cómo es que la comunidad se acerca a quienes todavía no han oído hablar de Cristo?
e. ¿Cómo es que la comunidad planifica y articula metas para orientar su labor misionera?
f. ¿Cómo es que el grupo evalúa su fidelidad a Cristo?

7. Dimensión Ministerial

Las pequeñas comunidades promueven la participación activa de sus miembros como colaboradores en el sacerdocio de Jesucristo. El principal ímpetu de todo ministerio es el reino de Dios.

a. ¿Cómo es que la comunidad promueve los dones que halla en cada uno de sus miembros?
b. ¿De qué manera son estos dones puestos al servicio del barrio y de la parroquia?
c. ¿Cómo es que los miembros de la comunidad se entrenan para ser ministros y líderes? ¿En la comunidad misma, en la parroquia, en la diócesis? ¿Qué tipo de entrenamiento se les ofrece?
d. ¿Todos los ministros trabajan en colaboración con el párroco y los otros agentes parroquiales de pastoral?
e. ¿Qué hacen para promover las vocaciones al sacerdocio, a la vida religiosa y a los demás ministerios parroquiales?
f. ¿De qué forma se respeta el papel de las mujeres en las comunidades?
g. ¿Cómo es que se trata de desarrollar, en la comunidad, un

compromiso serio con el ministerio?

h. ¿Qué medidas está tomando la comunidad para hacer que sus miembros abandonen la actitud de ser meros ayudantes del sacerdote o voluntarios parroquiales y se conviertan de hecho en colaboradores corresponsables de la vida de la Iglesia?

Sugerencia de Esquema para Reuniones

La estructura de estas reuniones depende de cada región del país, del tiempo litúrgico, del número de años que el grupo lleve junto, y cosas por el estilo.

Bienvenida

Oración de Alabanza y Cantos

Reflexión Bíblica o de Otro Tipo

Compartir en Grupo sobre la Reflexión (viendo como se aplica a su vida a la luz de la misión de la Iglesia)

Oración de los Fieles

Padre Nuestro

Anuncios y otros Asuntos de Interés para la Comunidad

Oración Final y Cantos

Hospitalidad

Notas

1. La experiencia de las pequeñas comunidades entre hispanos/latinos en los Estados Unidos es diferente a la experiencia latinoamericana de las comunidades de base. En los Estados Unidos, los hispanos catolicos son una minoría en un país protestante, víctimas frecuentes de la alienación cultural y lingüística. Puesto que los hispanos en Estados Unidos han forjado lazos íntimos entre su identidad cultural y sus expresiones de fe, las pequeñas comunidades eclesiales sirven para afirmar tanto la fe como la identidad cultural.

   La rica experiencia latinoamericana de las pequeñas comunidades de base, impulsada por Medellín, Puebla y Santo Domingo, seguirá enriqueciendo la discusión y la formación de la Iglesia en las Américas. Mas aún, la experiencia de las pequeñas comunidades eclesiales entre los católicos hispanos de Estados Unidos puede ayudar a otros en este país en la formación de comunidades similares.

2. Conferencia Nacional de Obispos Católicos. *Hispanic Presence: Challenge and Commitment* (Washington, D. C.: United States Catholic Conference Publishing Services, 1983); y *Plan Pastoral Nacional para el Ministerio Hispano* (Washington, D.C.: United States Catholic Conference Publishing Services, 1987).

3. Concilio Vaticano II. *Lumen Gentium. Constitución dogmática sobre la Iglesia*, 2-4. Efesios 2:18.

4. La expresión es de San Cipriano, en su *De oratione Dominica* 23, en: PL 4, 553; y es citada en la *Lumen Gentium*, 4.

5 "Vino a los suyos y los suyos no lo recibieron. Pero a quienes lo recibieron les dió poder de llegar a ser hijos de Dios. . ." (Jn 1:11-12).

6. Congregación para la Doctrina de la Fe. *Instrucción sobre la libertad cristiana y liberación* (Ciudad del Vaticano: Prensa Políglota Vaticana, 1986), 57.

7. Paulo VI. *Evangelii Nuntiandi* (1975). En el número 58, Paulo VI invita a las pequeñas comunidades a solidarizarse con la vida de la Iglesia, nutriéndose de sus enseñanzas y en unidad con sus pastores.
8. Hch 2:42-44: 2 Cor 13:13.
9. *Plan Pastoral Nacional para el Ministerio Hispano* (Washington, D.C.: United States Catholic Conference Publishing Services, 1987), 9-17.
10. Juan Pablo II. *Christifideles Laici* (1988), 26.
11. Concilio Vaticano II. *Sacrosanctum Concilium. Constitución sobre la Sagrada Liturgia*, 10.
12. Paulo VI, *Evangelii Nuntiandi* (1975), 20, 48. *Catecismo de la Iglesia Católica* (1994), 854, 1204-1207, 1679.
13. Vaticano II. *Ad Gentes.* Decreto sobre la actividad misionera de la Iglesia; y Juan Pablo II, *Redemptoris Missio* (1990).
14. *Catecismo de la Iglesia Católica* (Washington, D.C.: United States Catholic Conference Publishing Services, 1994), 1546.
15. Juan Pablo II. *Sobre la validez permanente del mandato misionero de la Iglesia* (1990), 51.
16. *Catecismo de la Iglesia Católica* (Washington, D.C.: United States Catholic Conference Publishing Services, 1994), 1268.